SCHOOL READINESS
for
PARENTS & CHILDREN
K–12

Children usually get along well with those whom they consider Mama's friends. When students recognize and observe that parents and teacher are on the same page, a positive explosion occurs!

This handbook is suitable for all learning environments!

Let's Keep Integrity in Our Classrooms!

By
Wanda J. Rice Prowell

RESOLVED-2010, LLC
Publishing House

www.resolved-2010.com

===================================
SCHOOL READINESS FOR PARENTS & CHILDREN, K–12
Just Look In The Book
===================================

Published by
ReSolved-2010 Publishing House
P.O. Box 82851
Conyers, Georgia 30013
(404) 966-5185
www.resolved-2010.com
resolved-2010@comcast.net

ISBN: 978-0-6155434-6-8
Printed in the United States of America

Copyright © 2011 by Wanda J. R. Prowell
All rights reserved. No part of this publication may be reproduced or transmitted in any form or by any means, electronic or mechanical, including photocopy, recording, or any information storage and retrieval system, without permission in writing from the copyright owner.

===================================
Library of Congress Control Number: 2011917684
===================================

Disclaimer

This book, *School Readiness for Parents and Children, K–12*, is not respresentative of, related to, sponsored by or affiliated with any school district or personnel. This book is an independent product of ReSolved-2010, LLC Publishing House and the information shared is the result of experience gained as an engaged parent, youth and community leader, scout leader, and long term early childhood entrepreneur and educator.

This publishing house and author do not promise or accept in any form the responsibility for your child's personal or academic growth, but we do believe that if these principles are applied through continuous parental engagement, your child will experience success.

Author, Wanda J.R. Prowell

ReSolved-2010, LLC
Publishing House

Dedication

I dedicate this book to all parents who have accepted the wonderful opportunity and challenge of parenting. Whether you are a parent by means of adoption, physical birth, or as a guardian, you have been entrusted with the most important task of our society, Parenting.

Maybe you are one of the parents who vowed that your child's life and career would exceed the opportunities of your own. I say, thank you! Perhaps your plans, finances, health, marital status, and employment were interrupted. Please be reminded that your most important attributes for the success of your child's future are those taught and practiced by you, not necessarily in the form of purchased tangible items.

I thank God for my parents who provided for seven of us children beginning in the late 1950s. I remember the coins tied in the four corners of a handkerchief for lunch and snack. Mother was a stay-at-home homemaker. She made breakfast every morning until we were able to assist her, and the aroma of dinner would meet us each afternoon as we got off the school bus. First, we completed our chores, then on to homework. Daddy and Mommy attended ALL of our school PTA meetings for the whole year, and most certainly during *"the high school years."* My parents were always concerned about our grades, but behavior, manners, and respect preceded all test and assignment scores. Our parents felt that if a child's discipline was in place, learning would be inevitable.

Parents are the first and most effective educators of a child. What is taught and modeled in the home becomes foundational. It remains for life: generations through generations. As adults, we have learned protocol, but it is at home that our true values are displayed. I mean the true character that arises when guests are not over.

Our parents taught us the importance of flexibility as required to withstand life's uncertainties. They would echo "keep your mind on what you are doing," which meant staying focused. They provided all that we needed and some of what we wanted. They were leaders in the home. If a problem arose at school or anywhere, Daddy would go down to the school and speak to the appropriate person, respectfully. He never shifted those issues on to us as children. He felt that children should stay in their place and the adults should lead as adults.

We are living in an unstable economy today. Our children are crying for foundational guidance and survival skills that will complement formal education. Parents, YOUR presence and involvement will make the difference in every aspect of your child's life!

Thank you for valuing the efforts made toward school readiness and preparation for parents and children K–12.

School Readiness for Parents and Children, K–12
(Suitable for all learning environments)

Table of Contents

Disclaimer iii

Dedication v

About the Book xiii

Chapter 1: Home Is Where the Heart Is 1

Chapter 2: Behavioral Expectations for Effective Learning 9

Chapter 3: Homework, a Family Effort 25

Chapter 4: The School Handbook 31

Chapter 5: Who Am I? 41

Chapter 6: Count Up the Cost: Social Laws.........47

Chapter 7: Parents: The Primary Career Coach 53

Chapter 8: Leadership in Action, Graduation 65

Your Career Summary: Conclusion 73

About the Author 81

Appendix 85

Parent Assessment
School Readiness for Parents and Children, K–12
(Suitable for all learning environments)

Please read each item below and write <u>yes</u> or <u>no</u> on each blank line as it applies to you.

Is This Book for Your Family?

____ Do you want your child to be someone of influence?

____ Do you feel that your child's social and employability skills are just as important as academic skills?

____ Do you want your child to attract positive, helpful people?

_____ Do you value someone who has a good reputation?

_____ Do you believe that friends define your character?

_____ Do you feel that it is okay to practice having the last word?

_____ Do you believe that the parent's participation influences the respect given to the child?

_____ Do you believe that evil communication corrupts good manners?

_____ Is rest important to you?

_____ Do you feel that the need to "Fit-in" and Acceptance are important parent and child discussion topics?

** Please settle for nothing less than an A+

Give yourself 10 points for each "yes."

About the Book

I remember seeing a preschool's logo that read, "Find Grandma's Love at Knee Cole's Learning Center." Grandma's Love was the pitch. The term "Grandma" did not necessarily refer to the biological grandmother, but to the character which society had accepted as being a responsible, caring and sharing, mature, aged lady. This character may describe a calm, loving personality, but please remember that "Grandma was no pushover!" She would give you her last, but accepted no disrespect. Maybe this is how the name "Big Mama" came into being. There were many cases when Grandma or Big Mama may have been in error, but because of the love she had given to everyone, her motives were never challenged because of her commitment to the family. Keep this in mind as you reminisce about the mobility of today's families in our society. It is not like back in the days when the married/single parents could always count on the assistance of extended family members and Grandma/Big Mama. Childcare assistants were never a danger or worry. The children were always happy and safe. Sometimes the childcare hours were for a few hours, at other times, maybe overnight.

Parents and Big Mama began preparing the children for school very early. Hear me now: preparing children for school did not necessarily refer to all academic preparation. Many households referred to "academic preparation" as secondary school preparation. Parents were fully committed to instilling a sense of value and fundamental commitment within their children that expressed the uniqueness of their family to the public. These values would distinguish or set them apart from the "other folks." Children left home with a sense of pride representing their parents, family, church, and the community in which they lived.

About the Book

Five Major Areas of Family Respect and Family Pride

- *Elders, Family & Community*—Acknowledge verbal respect, visible respect.

- *Household Accountability*—Chores, neat organizational skills, mutual respect for belongings. No sloppy work, strive to do it well!

- *Moral and Spiritual Accountability*—Character development. Certain actions were not acceptable regardless of others. Family worship and divine guidance. Never give up!

- *Self-respect and Personal Accountability*—Love yourself! Self value. Choose friends who value you and your values and beliefs.

- *Finally, Academic Accountability*—Parental engagement and supervision for school accountability and academic success. Parents personally knew every adult who was responsible for their child(ren). They made learning fun while building relationships. They oversaw test reviews, homework, class projects, school books being brought home, and supplies used and carried to school. As a parent, what would be your preference of the statements below? Which do you deem as being most important?

My child is an "A" student and always completes his/her work.

OR

I encourage my child to complete assignments and get an "A," but is my child respectful and does he/she allow other students to work without interruption?

If "knowledge" is power," then "character" must be—KEY.

Knowledge Gets the Job, Character Keeps the Job!

Grandmas are wonderful and many of them are God sent, but parents are given the Godly and legal authority to develop wonderful young men and women. Our

About the Book

community leaders, churches, community centers, libraries, school districts, and community health organizations all partner to provide parents the available resources to assist in school readiness skills and educational maintenance. Begin "EARLY," dig deep, set priorities, get involved, and have realistic age-appropriate expectations for your child(ren).

Chapter ONE

Home Is Where the Heart Is

Home is where the heart is. For a child, this primary location houses everything of value and of utmost importance. A house refers to a construction or place that provides him/her shelter and protection from the weather, sometimes called a "roof over your head." A *home* is sometimes characterized by the type of atmosphere within the house such as the social, emotional, and intellectual interaction of the people living there. In various relationship classes, strong discussions are developed as points of view are aired concerning the greater or lesser importance of a house vs. a home.

However the discussion goes, it is important that all who are assigned to children understand that the living conditions of each child echo the reality of that child's school day. If the caregiver is sensitive to the needs of the child, he/she will lend a *third ear* to hear the *emotions and heart of the child* as well as see the obvious behavior. You would think that the older the child, the clearer the avenues of communication would be: not so. Older children may tend to remain silent to avoid scandals or embarrassments. A younger child may begin crying and say the problem is something totally different and not disclose what he/she is really feeling. My point is, whether you are working with a kindergartner or high schooler, both cases require a high level of professionalism and respect for the child as you are able to project genuine concern and care, as opposed to just digging for facts.

Who Is Abraham Maslow?

First, I will share that he was a psychologist who believed that all humans had certain basic *"needs."* Now if you teach high schoolers in any form, you know to pause here for a second and let this term *"need"* be digested before moving on. The essence of this statement is to give you a moment to realistically differentiate a *"need"* from a *"want."* Many will agree that it was the *"wants"* of many individuals in our society that contributed to our present-day economy.

Wants

Wants simply refer to "wants," which *are desires for something that is not life threatening nor health challenging.* Wants soothe our emotions, temporarily. Soon afterward, we will want something else to replace the first want. This may go on continuously for all age groups. Wants compared to human needs could be similar to how our body craves fats and carbohydrates, the good stuff that we do not need.

Essential Question #1:

If "wants" are items we do not need and contribute to excessive spending, why do parents allow themselves to become stressed in trying to supply the wants of their children?

Essential Question #2:

Also, if the parent warrants purchasing some of the wants, why would they not be attached to a form of reward system of achievement?

Lawrence Kohlberg was another child psychologist who addressed the stages of moral development and moral reasoning. He believed that it was detrimental to the child to reward negative behavior. Parents must incorporate some form of discipline (not punishment) and it should begin as early as the toddler stage. Punishment refers to correcting only, whereas discipline refers to teaching and correcting. Therefore, by school age, each K–12 student will already understand the *"Not Burger King Platform,"* which is the "no tolerance" for *"Having It Your Way Syndrome."* This is not an opportunity for the teacher or parent to become careless or not thoughtful, but simply an opportunity to highlight the type of characteristic desired to move students forward in learning and demonstrating good decision-making skills.

Eric Erickson believed that if a development skill is not learned and demonstrated during a child's early years, although the individual may increase in his/her chronological age, the actions displayed for that maturation age would remain the same.

Parents, educators, and mentors view this ***need*** as being an awesome responsibility to firmly and lovingly hold individuals accountable as we coach them in how to process decision-making skills through "real life—daily events."

Needs

Need simply refers to "a need," (nothing sexual), simply a *necessity that the individual "must have" for survival.* This is by no means optional and it should *never be used as rewards for any purpose.* Otherwise, it may be categorized as an abusive behavior with legal consequences. There are five categories of human needs according to Abraham Maslow: Physical Needs, Safety and Security Needs, Love and Acceptance Needs, Esteem Needs and Self-Actualization Needs. Hierarchy of need refers to the levels of need beginning with the lowest level as being the most important for basic human survival. As parents, educators, and caregivers, we all agree that we do not just want our children to survive, we want them to exceed survival, we want them to become winners, leaders for their families as well as our communities, state, and our world. If all this is true, then we must offer our children beyond Level 1, Physical Needs.

Hierarchy of Needs for Everyone

Level 5—Self-Actualization Needs
(Reached your personal goal and are now ready to help others)

Level 4—Esteem Needs
(Self-respect & respect for others)

Level 3—Love and Acceptance Needs
(Affection & Approval—from family first)

Level 2—Safety and Security Needs
(Free from danger, financial security)

Level 1—Physical Needs

Can you imagine how a child would feel who had experienced only Level 1 and hearing speakers speaking on planning his/her career? The same would be true for any of the different levels of need. The important fact to remember is *"everyone has needs."* We must examine our motive for the decisions that we are making on behalf of our child (ren). Needs vs. Wants?

Essential Question #3?

Do we allow our childhood emotions to prevent us from making the decision of need for the child? Are you easily affected by the child's response?

Essential Question #4

Am I walking through the decision-making process with my children or am I guilty of throwing them problems and expecting them to solve those problems independently, without guidance?

I have witnessed parents who were negligent in coaching their students with decision-making skills throughout, but suddenly before midterm or senior exam they withdrew their guidance. The child was completely lost. Children's 18th birthday will not prove them competent but time well spent with accountability will.

Parents have to do… what they
do not… want to do now,
So their child… will leave home with…
what they need later!

Chapter One will remain your foundational chapter throughout this book. For every situation, please access it and determine if a "need" or a "want" is involved and decide how you can create teachable moments for a successful future. Remember that discipline is teaching plus correcting and punishment is correcting only. Building a positive relationship with your child is key. Do not be afraid to give tough love while yet saying "I am sorry" and "I love you."

Chapter TWO

Behavioral Expectations for Effective Learning
(Back To Basics: Good Manners & Social Skills)

B ack to basic skills is a familiar term that is used quite frequently. Chapter Two will analyze various aspects of the term "respect" and how the lack of it can alter the school environment. Some of the aspects of respect for the school environment include: In-house bullying, obedience/following instructions, courteous/polite behavior, work ethics/distractions, career preparation, and appropriate mealtime behavior.

In-House Bullying

I cannot tell you how important it is that the parent is actively engaged from the toddler stage in modeling and enforcing siblings' nurturing and caring for each other. Many parents or guardians may choose to ignore negative communication and physical interaction of siblings and feel that it is part of toughening up to deal with the real world. Each individual is born with a unique personality. Some are highly aggressive and others may be shy. Children's confidence and self-esteem are damaged when they are left to fend for themselves. There should be some in-house rules to always be respected. With all the concerns in our country today regarding school bullying, a horrible fact is that some children do not feel safe and secure at home. Adults must take the lead in producing a loving environment at home. Learning for careers will never take place if a child's emotions do not feel loved and are not respected and secure. A happy, loving, and safe family is easy to recognize away from home. If there are siblings with special needs, the parent has a greater responsibility to make certain that all family members understand and demonstrate the concept of love, care, and support in the home first. It is very painful to observe siblings ignoring each other in public: Examples: speaking harsh words and ignoring the interaction of a special needs sibling who is smiling and trying to communicate. Youngsters may ignore their handicapped siblings at school because they are embarrassed by them.

The Expectation for Employability Skills

As we continue to guide students into a successful future, we are reminded of the importance of personal skills as shared by John Rosemond. Rosemond wrote "Four hundred respondents were asked to rate their biggest disappointment when it came to filling jobs. The biggest problem was hires who lack the ability/willingness to follow directions. The biggest disappointments were punctuality, positive attitude, ambition, and honesty. The survey draws no conclusion, but I'll offer one: It would appear that today's parents would do well to focus less on getting their children into gifted and talented programs and focus more on teaching them manners, respect for others, responsibility and other basic character values. As my wife and I often told our children as they were growing up, there are more than a few geniuses in this world who are failures. But, there are very few people who respect other people and their property and have proper social skills who fail, regardless of IQ." *www.rosemond.com/parenting.*

Obedience/Body Language

Obedience and body language are a very critical aspect of respecting the learning environment. What makes this aspect so critical is the showcasing of this behavior to make or break the entire learning expectation. There are times in our lives when everyone at some time is in opposition to a direction given. It is the manner in which we respond to the opposition that determines the outcome. It is okay to disagree, but do it respectfully. There should be communication between only you and that person, no negative body language, and, for example, no throwing of objects. These are similar guidelines used in conflict resolution for professional careers. Keep the voice tone low and speak respectfully to the person with whom you are in opposition. Never make a scene, throw objects, or damage property; this will get you a negative evaluation and perhaps terminated—fired!

A very good observation to keep in mind is to not be afraid to let your positive personality shine. It is instantly attractive and therefore easily recognized. Be assertive! Volunteer to do the extras. You will be remembered and a letter of recommendation will be a breeze. Make it work for you.

Work Ethics

Often the teacher will ask the class to settle down, continue to work, or say "You are too loud." Students usually respond by saying, "I'm doing my work." The teacher already understands that students may have various learning styles, meaning some may be able to multi-task and talk while working and other students may not. The learning expectation is that "no child is left behind" and every student should have the opportunity to learn and retain knowledge uninterrupted.

Essential Question #5

How does my child's school behavior affect his/her future careers?

For the most part, just getting the class work completed is not satisfactory. Did the student retain the information and is he/she able to paraphrase a summary of all the facts? For example:

1. Is the assignment completed correctly?

2. Is the student able to compare, analyze, discuss, and give examples of principles and concepts

of the completed assignment and make real life connections?

I am afraid that many times, the answer is "no." This type of behavior contributes to low test scores because of the lack of concentration and may also cause failure in other students by interrupting and causing others to not be able to focus.

Whether the student completed the assignment correctly or not is irrelevant to the other students and to disrespect of the learning environment.

Courtesy/Politeness

Your most important fact: A lot of young people do feel that *please, excuse me, I'm sorry, thank you, yes/no ma'am, yes/no sir* are all old fashioned, not "cool," and nobody says them anymore. This could be the furthest from the truth. Truth is, because of this inverted psychology that they want you to believe, those who process and demonstrate these qualities are often highly admired and easily recognized. Businesses and industries are seeking applicants who showcase "professionalism." Isn't it amazing how that term changes from one environment to the next? Great manners and work ethics describe professionalism. Please discuss the importance of these jewels with your children and get the whole family involved by saying them routinely to each other, and watch your young person begin attracting professional admiration. Character does count!

Students' Dress Code/Appearance

Fashion appears to be everything to students and I must admit that I am not certain if the stress comes from personal acceptance or wanting the acclamation of peers and others. It is important to some students to dress in the latest fashions. To other students, it is important that they wear the latest fashions to school. Yet, there remain students who are not intrigued by fashion stress at all. There are students who take the position of criticizing other students' clothing and apparel with the intent to embarrass. The point is, this may be a good time to address as parents your value system for such behavior and how unpredictable our economy is right now—and, most importantly, how students' behavior could affect school attendance and career preparation for other students.

Throughout the school year, students will have an opportunity to attend various events which require specific types of attire. Regardless of the occasion, several students from various socio-economic backgrounds will wear *an inappropriate* garment with a name brand label rather than *an appropriate* garment with a no-name brand label. Take some time, as a family activity, to explore selecting appropriate clothing for your events. Please highlight the words "private time." Discuss them as they relate to after-school and after-work attire.

Examples of various attire (type of clothing to wear)

- *School dress for everyday class*—Follow the guidelines of the School Student Handbook dress code.

- *School dress special event*—Field trips, school trips, class presentations, school day events.

- *Sports/Extracurricular activities*—Dress in appropriate uniform.

- *Formal/Semi formal/Casual events*—Banquets, balls, proms, etc.

Behavioral Expectations for Effective Learning

- Most importantly, parents are to share these discussions with their child/young adult so that he/she will understand and hear the information from the voice of their parent and not feel personally hindered by school sponsors. This would be a good time for your children to show off their family pride by dressing appropriately.

Needs Apparel

This is the area where assistance may be needed. Don't be afraid or embarrassed to get the correct support garments for your young adult. You may call leading department stores for men/boys and juniors/women for appropriate support undergarments: Jocks, slips, fitted bras, etc. As your child progresses in school, business and career days will become more frequent. Every young man should have a tie, dark shoes, dress shirt (white is good if you only get one color) and dark pants. Nothing has to be brand new. Young ladies will need a dark skirt or dress not more than two inches above the knee, and dark shoes. Always discuss and get approval from your child's teacher as early as possible. Basic maternity wear would allow your expectant teen free movement during the school day and adequate coverage throughout her day.

If you should need assistance, always make an appointment with the guidance counselor to learn what type of help may be available.

School Supplies

First, the school supplies do not have to be brand new. Please make contact with the teacher and/or counselor to determine the supply list for your child as soon as possible. You are also able to communicate any hardship in getting the supplies. Once supplies have been obtained, review the importance of care, maintenance, and proper utilization of supplies. Help children to realize the economic value and replacement cost of the products. For example: A bottle of glue may cost $1.00 but the replacement cost and drive to the store will cost so much more. Moreover, there should be no excuse for not completing the project assignment.

Family Meals at the Dinner Table

Family meals at the dinner table are so important. Students are eager to showcase their family pride in

Behavioral Expectations for Effective Learning

eating together at the table as a family. Some students say that they have a wonderful and beautifully decorated dining room but it is usually for company and for special occasions. If truth be told, there are important functions of eating at the family table that contribute to a child's school day.

1. Family meals allow parents to observe mealtime manners and give friendly suggestions for correction. It is very difficult for a child to understand and demonstrate good table manner skills in public when he/she is not engaged at home.

2. Eating relaxes the child, therefore conversation becomes easy. It is amazing the information that will come forth just by the parent asking, "How was your day?"

3. Opportunity to offer thanks and to discuss healthy choices. I understand that family schedules may not allow whole family dining on a daily basis, but please recognize the importance of it and modify your schedule to include as many as possible. Some basic mealtime manners

should include: not throwing food, using a napkin, keeping your food on your plate, leaving your place setting clean and throwing away the trash, pushing your chair up, not engaging in horseplay, never putting your hand in someone else's plate or taking their food.

Behavioral Expectations for Effective Learning

Let's Think About It
Homework/Class work

True/False

1. Children are more successful when parents are involved. _____

2. Parents may not understand the subject area but may still be able to give support. _____

3. Children must have a good learning environment at home to study and complete assignments. _____

4. A short rest and a wake-up snack may be given immediately after school. _____

5. Parents should review homework assignments, projects, and test reviews when possible. _____

6. Parents are responsible for demonstrating proper leadership skills in the home. Settle the dispute

or conflict in the home without feeding the bully. Bullying begins in the home. Get the help you need and do not allow this behavior to transfer into the classroom and school. Don't leave your other, innocent children helpless. _____

7. Parents should establish household guidelines for respecting property of siblings and household goods. _____

8. Parents should define, explain, and engage students in the practice of demonstrating understanding of the terms: stop, listen, quiet, no, hands to self, taking, please, sit down. _____

9. Parents should insist that children maintain basic/orderly work, and the sleeping or eating area (not throwing garbage on floor, putting up the meal tray, pushing chairs up, handling books and property with care.) _____

10. Parents should discuss the relationship between dress code and employment. Dress for the occasion vs. name brand and cost. _____

Behavioral Expectations for Effective Learning

11. Parents should discourage and not tolerate profanity. It displays anger, lack of self-control, zero vocabulary, disrespect, low self-esteem to the child, and ignorance. _____

Society has multiple answers for why children and/or parents should not be expected to comply with the above descriptions. Unfortunately, when circumstances arise where law enforcement becomes involved, the above restrictions or suggestions may seem mild. Prison behavioral modifications are NOT as those in our schools, which are very limited or may not exist at all. Children, parents, visitors, and friends are expected to comply with all law enforcement regulations, with no exceptions: Strict bedtime, uniform worn correctly, limited menu, meal schedule, lights out, restricted movement, NO FORM of disrespect tolerated. What are your thoughts? Are the above expectations truly cruel and not rational for preparing our children for the real world?

Chapter THREE

Homework, a Family Effort!

We all understand that the report card or progress report is a reflection of completed and accurate homework. A few years ago much emphasis was placed on homework. Homework grades were an important reflection of a student's total school performance. I can remember some serious punishment for failure to complete and turn in the work the next day. If an assigned project required glue and the family did not have any, mothers would use any sticky substance from the kitchen that could be used as a substitute, and food coloring or Kool-Aid was used to color projects. Whatever the case was, everyone was creative in working together for the student's success. Report card day was a celebration because it was truly a reflection of the student's progress, since parents and older siblings would not dare do the assignment, but would supervise, assist, and review.

> *Supervise*—Make certain the child understood the assignment, stayed focused, and worked.
>
> *Assist*—Give examples, demonstrations, and models of the correct answer or procedure(s).
>
> *Review*—Do not take the child's word for completion only, but review the work for completion, correctness, and memory.

What is so amazing about all of this is that the 1960's through the 1970's were a very rough period economically for most uneducated, low income families. As I remember, parent support was at its peak. Parents readily vocalized to their children and in front of the teacher, respectfully, that because they were uneducated themselves, they demanded that their children must get their homework and classwork. They were very clear in not accepting one without the other: Good Grades and Good Manners! Some parents made "Good Manners" the priority.

Present-Day America

From reading the above scenario, I must ask: Is the economy to blame for the status of education and morality? We must admit, there is an overwhelming number of educated, professional, and entrepreneurial parents with multiple degrees. What is it about our household culture that has produced, for the vast majority, underachievers from what appears to be healthy, well-groomed children?

It amazes me how healthy, special needs children put forth their greatest effort and excel. I have noticed over the years that whether the child is physically handicapped or economically disadvantaged, his/her character is the determining factor. When a child's attitude is in the right place, then retaining the knowledge is easier and results in leaders of authority.

Homework, a Family Effort

We are living in a fast-paced society with pleasure and comforts because of many answered prayers of our ancestors. When it comes to homework and academic success, parents and guardians cannot assume children or young adults share the same learning styles. It is very important that you as a parent or guardian take the time to review a learning style web site below and take the free survey test to determine your child's learning style and to educate yourself in understanding the type and necessity of assistance you should give.

Web Site Resources

What's Your Learning Style? *http://people.usd. edu/~bwjames/tut/learning-style/*

Personal Learning Style Survey *http://people.usd. edu/~bwjames/tut/learning-style/stylest.html*

Three Types of Learning Styles:

Educators were taught and understand the importance of identifying a student's learning style. Educators are required to survey and examine their own personal learning style, at the beginning of each school year, so that they are able to relate to and communicate the needs of the students. It is obvious that a teaching and learning strategy must be activated for overall student success. Once the various learning styles have been examined and recognized, then the teacher is able to meet the need of his/her students. Therefore, when parents

Homework, a Family Effort!

understand this same concept, they are now able to get the whole family involved to effectively assist the child for academic success.

Example: Calling spelling words out, flash cards, getting a playback recorder, creating answer songs, etc.

> *Visual Learner*—This individual learns from seeing the lesson demonstrated: printed word, flash cards, color-coded cards, highlighter, posters, charts, movie, etc.
>
> *Auditory Learner*—This individual learns from hearing. Read out loud, wants others to read information out loud or record questions and statements—play back, songs, demonstrated role-play. Create answers or jog memory with a song or rap.
>
> *Kinesthetic Learner/Tactile Learner*—This individual learns through touching, demonstrating, experiments, lots of labs, dance & movement.

Chapter FOUR

The School Handbook
Just Look In The Book
(Handbook)

This session is written in general terms and may not represent your specific location. However, it includes enough information to educate parents of the seriousness of their support and involvement with the total educating process. The following information is very compatible to multiple districts and I strongly encourage you to be proactive in speaking to your school professionals.

School districts do a great job in compiling the policy manuals/parent handbooks and having them ready for distribution the first week of school. Due to the increased diversity of communities, school policies throughout our country, manuals, and handbooks were continuously modified to meet the demanding needs of each school day. Therefore, in an effort to ensure students' understanding of the policy handbook, administrators found it necessary to have the classroom teacher not only issue each student a district policy student handbook, but also discuss and review it in the classroom for clarity. After this, students were asked to return all parent signature sheets from the handbook, with the parent signature, back to the teacher. Many parents did read and discuss the policy handbook with their children, others neither signed nor returned all necessary papers; however, some parents chose to quickly sign the papers, without reading or discussing them, assuming that all rules and regulations were the same as the previous year. Several other students believed that if their parents did not sign or return the sheet, they as students could not be held accountable for their actions. Failing to read the policy handbook meant that parents did not have a clue to the school regulations nor the discipline associated with offenses. These failures created a void in the communication between school and parents. It is impossible to

The School Handbook

create a support system and set student expectation when the objectives (handbook rules) are not acknowledged or recognized.

Let us identify some sections of the student handbook and *highlight* the topic to briefly explain some important facts. Please be reminded that this is not conclusive and does not in any way replace the details of the District Policy for the Student Handbook. Here are some sections:

School Calendar, Extracurricular Regulations, Attendance Policy, Bus Transportation, Check-in and Check-out Procedures, Clubs and Organizations, Counseling Service, Deliveries, Disciplinary Code of Conduct, Drivers' Education, Gifted Education, Grading System, Graduation Requirements, Hall Behavior, College Grants & Scholarships, I-parent, Student Internet Usage, JROTC, Learning Support Services, Locker Inspection, Lost and Found, Student Makeup Work, Medication/Illness, Open Campus Classes, Parent Advisory Council, Online Classes, Post-Secondary Options, Release of Information, Report Cards, Technology Academy, School Closing, School Food Service/Meal Prices, School Hours of Operation, Student Searches/Interrogations/Surveillance, Student Complaints and Grievances, Student

Support Services, Summer School/Credit Recovery, Substance Abuse, Telephone/Cell Phones, Testing Dates, Test Preparation Information, Textbook/Library Books, Visitors, and Forms.

Round Table Parent and Children-Family Meeting

These can take place at the kitchen table, sofa in the living room, etc.

Examples of Parent Signature Forms: Code of Conduct and Attendance, Student Affirmation Form, Code of Conduct Contract, Extracurricular Participation, Acceptable Use Agreement for Internet, Request for School Staff to Administer Medication, Student Photo Release and Work Release, Parent/Student/School Compact-Contact.

Parents are to read and discuss the handbook information with the student. Make certain the rules are clear and the consequences are understood, no exceptions. Please be certain to explain that the District has already approved the handbook. The teacher and staff are not responsible for the rules but must enforce them. Obedience is key for a successful day and career!

Highlights from the Parent/Student Handbook

The information in this section does not represent the entire student handbook. It only gives parents at a glance notice of the various topics addressed. Please refer to your handbook for a complete description of details. Brief descriptions are provided below to prompt interest.

a. *Meals—NO LUNCH MONEY?*—Change in income, or just moved? Talk with your principal immediately!

b. *Attendance policy*—Attendance is important for success. Keep a current telephone number on file for your parent call notice, check I-Parent constantly for tardiness.

c. *Deliveries*—Read your handbook! Many schools do not allow any deliveries, or stuffed animals, balloons, flowers, etc. during the school day.

d. *Discipline code of conduct*—Proof that the handbook was issued to and discussed with the parent.

e. *Grading system*—It is always a good idea to notify the school district that you are moving to verify dates and required documents, district block style so students will have no loss of credit. If possible speak with your child's counselor to understand the best time to transfer. Request to have students' letter grades transferred if possible. 65 may be an "F" in some states, and a **"D"** in others.

f. *Graduation requirements*—Parents should not leave everything up to the counselor, but because they know their children better than anybody else, they should coach and lead them early to future goals. Parents should guide them in grade transfers, including online courses, and should retain report cards and all graded work. Reward their hard work.

g. *Hall behavior*—The handbook describes the expectation for orderly conduct in the hall. It is during this time that professionalism and career expectations are highlighted. No derogatory language, vandalizing walls or school property, yelling, jumping, music, singing, dress code violation, kissing, whole body hugs, fighting, whole body touching, or back riding. School is fun but yet a professional environment preparing students for college and careers.

h. *I-parent*—Code issued to parent to immediately track on your home computer your child's tardiness, absences, grades, and behavior.

i. *Student makeup work*—Outlines what is approved for makeup work and the students' responsibility for getting it completed and the time frame involved.

j. *Medication/illness*—Whether the student has a chronic illness or just needs a Tylenol, this form must be completed and forwarded to the school nurse.

k. *Report cards*—A parent should mandate and review report cards. These are legal documents and joint-custody parents are held responsible.

l. *School closing*—Children should never be dropped off at school when the building is closed. This is a legal child safety matter for all parents.

m. *Child-related restrictions*—These can be very harmful to children's health. Please communicate with the teacher or nurse as needed. Make certain that meal arrangements are cleared. Food smells very tasty during mealtime when everyone is hungry.

n. *School hours of operation*—No child regardless of age is allowed to be on school property unsupervised. Physical assault, violation, and youthful lust could have legal repercussions.

o. *Student searches/interrogations/and surveillance*—If authorities are in doubt, the law will be executed to the fullest. Warn students to monitor items they will be held responsible for in their possession, including those in their locker. Do not share lockers with anyone and keep yours locked.

p. *Telephone/cell phones*—Please read this section thoroughly in the handbook. Phones are not allowed to be out in the classroom. Parents should not call students during class time. It interrupts their learning and, worst case, the student is not in a private environment to handle disappointing news in the classroom. If this should be the case, call the counselor or school secretary and ask them to come and not expect a student to drive home after receiving drastic, alarming news. Secondly, discuss and warn your student of the laws that regulate taking pictures of anyone with his/her cell phone. Accept the responsibility for letting others use the phone. Because cell phones are not allowed in the classroom and students are not given additional teacher instruction for not taking pictures, students could well be accountable to law enforcement for Internet usage.

3-Part Essential Question #6

What are your and your child's ultimate goal for this year? What is your plan for making it happen? What are some personal assessments for a successful school year?

Chapter FIVE

Who Am I?
(Fit In At All Cost?)

This may be a good time to refer back to Chapter One and refresh your memory of Abraham Maslow's hierarchy of eight needs for all humans. Level 3 Needs refer to the need for love and acceptance (affection & approval—from family first) and Level 4 Needs refer to the esteem of parents and children K–12. These two levels will make or break a student, especially middle and high school. This is a time when peer pressure peaks. The crucial fact is that parents may have been very supportive in earlier years, but by now the family structure has changed. Whether caused by death, separation, new job schedule, illness, accidents, relocating, or whatever it may be. This is by no means the time for parents to react in denial by embracing the thought of higher-level parenting and showcasing it by giving your teen assumed, unrealistic expectations beyond their maturity level.

Consistency is "Key" here. So many entities encompass the maturity level of your high school student. For example: academic decisions; social decisions; sexuality decisions; appearance—dress; professional disposition & communication skills—language/profanity; theft; attendance—cut classes; physical altercation; class clown; drugs & alcohol. Students may behave well in the surrounding of their homes or in their local churches. The ultimate goal for parents, caregivers, and mentors is to inspire youth to develop self-disciplinary skills where they not only experience personal gratification for themselves, but also for the people they hold dear, such as family. All humans were created to have and desire a sense of belonging, in most cases with family, friends, even pets. When students choose friends of similar values (not based on money) such as academics, respect & manners, career goals, character, and teamwork, this type of positive relationship becomes obvious to everyone because of the positive impact it has made for the betterment of the person.

In an effort to be called friendly, loving, kind, sweet, wonderful, and "cool," popular students may begin to participate in undesirable groups and actions to just fit in. If home is crazy (as they would say) they will seek approval elsewhere. Sometimes homes could be apparently fine and still parents may become curious about certain actions. You as parents must lean in closer to your child/teen. This will require a higher level of thinking to create engagement strategies for you and your child/teen and/or teen friends. Example: supervised events, casual home activities, movies, cookouts, career planning, cooking, fishing, etc. with the other friends and parents you are now getting to know. This is hard work and time consuming! Just shouting "No,"... "Stay away from,"... "I better not catch you"... will not bring you a positive response! Children will rebel and use every school hour as an opportunity to connect. As parents you want to counteract the disturbance by putting your minds together to plan not just for now, but to make a future connection. Parents must work together! What does your child show interest in?

Whether in kindergarten or high school, this answer will be the foundation for your strategies.

Becoming involved in youth leadership programs and church youth groups is "Key." If you choose to join your child's youth organization, you may learn that activities are already planned and some expense has already been taken into consideration. What they need are volunteers to help develop and supervise their activities, BINGO! Get involved! You will learn so much about what is going on in the streets as well as home that will engage you and your child/teen.

I understand that a lot has been said regarding the bully, one who approaches the innocent child and violates him/her for no reason. This should not take place or be enjoyed by observers in any form. There are quiet, isolated students at school who are not challenged at all by anyone because they do not care about being laughed at about their clothes, shoes, hairstyle or cut, glasses, or having to eat alone. They have strong family ties and KNOW who they are! These students are not overwhelmed by trying to fit in! Their positive self-esteem is so high among family members that it overflows into their student and teacher relationship, which results in great student participation and excellent grades. The expectation for all students should be to "fit in" for classroom inclusion and making good grades. What an excellent way to exemplify your family pride away from home!

Good Rules of Thumb:

1. Think Before Acting/Participating.

2. Ask: Is This My Thought or Am I Following Someone Else's Thought?

3. Is It Worth the Consequence?

4. How Will This Affect My Family Financially?

5. How Will the Consequences Affect Me Now and Later?

Chapter SIX

Count Up the Cost: Social Laws
(Social Laws/Parent Orientation)

Almost all schools have a school orientation at the beginning of the school year. School orientation is the most important aspect of the school year. All parents and students who are not able to attend the initial school opening orientation should have the opportunity to complete an orientation during student registration. As a result of this school opening orientation, parents can immediately determine whether a student's offense is considered an "In-House" or "Out-of-House" offense and understand the recommended disposition/consequence.

Out-of-House Offense—Consequences beyond the authority of the school building. Criminal action—citizen arrest; a downtown issue. Fines and possible serving time, etc.

In-House Offense—Consequences issued at the school level. No criminal action applies.

School District/Building Policy

It is very important that parents read and understand the recommended disposition/consequences listed in the parent handbook. The school parent handbook is your legal resource guide for a successful school year. It presents resource guidance as it refers to acceptable and unacceptable characteristics at school. I believe that proof of parental involvement will soon become required documents from the custodial parents. As in any fire safety or first aid class, prevention and being proactive is the most effective strategy. Parents and teachers are accepting the challenge to work together for the success of the student (s).

These are some of the examples of forms parents may be asked to read, sign, and return to the school: Medication Health & Distribution Form, Medical Release Form, Code of Conduct, School Lunch, Child Release/Pickup, and others to be addressed in various sections of this book.

Family Project
RIGHTS AND RESPONSIBILITIES OF TEENAGER UNDER LAW

(Call your local Office of the District Attorney to acquire a copy for your state.)

Take this opportunity to call your local law enforcement agency and ask them for guidance in educating your group of young people (your child & some friends, church group, or community group) on the various social laws and how they can interrupt what appears to be a promising career.

Remember the word "PROactive." It is amazing how often children and teens respond to an instruction by saying: "Oh, yes, I got it." Teenagers will go on and on saying: "Yes, yes," and would not have heard a word you said because their minds were in a different place while you were talking to them. We must help them "HEAR CLEARLY," "COMPREHEND," and "UNDERSTAND" the "consequence" before the misbehavior or offense occurs. This may be done by simply asking them to restate what you have said to them or asking them to interpret the meaning.

Consider These Common Topics To Which They Often Respond "MY BAD."

How Do You Feel Law Enforcement Will Respond To the Following?

- Inappropriate touching
- Public cussing
- Threatening
- In your face
- Lying
- Spreading rumors/lies
- Bullying
- Cheating
- Stealing, taking without permission
- Invasion of privacy, purse, desk, book bags
- Vandalism
- Indecent, public exposure

Count Up the Cost: Social Laws

- Aggravated assault
- Criminals—Citizen arrest; a downtown issue. Fines and possible serving time
- Non-criminal Issues—building and county policies
- Leaving campus
- Turning gas or electric stoves on for laughs

You Better THINK!

Let's Turn It Around... Old School Motivations

- Don't burn the bridges you may have to cross.
- The best apology is to not do it.
- Once a task has begun, never leave it until it is done. Be the laborer, great or small, do it well or not at all.
- Laughing catches!
- God doesn't like ugly.
- Beauty is as beauty does!

- Play now... PAY LATER!

- No pain... NO GAIN!

- It's okay to be without money sometimes—just use what you have wisely!

- One man's trash is another man's treasure.

- Life is 10% what happens to me, 90% how I react to it!

- Wise is the person who fortifies his life with the right friendships.

- It is better to be alone than in the wrong company.

- There is a king inside all of us. Which one we address determines who will respond.

- True love is expressed with your heart, but understood with your head.

- Your friends will either make you lap water like a dog or soar like an eagle.

Chapter SEVEN

Parents: The Primary Career Coach

Parents are the first and most important educators of a child. This statement goes beyond academic expectation; it is the foundational core which motivates a child to excel. I have experienced numerous hours working with early learners and often I would hear them say repeatedly, "My mommy said," and "My daddy said." My point is that children believe and trust their parents. It is very crucial that parents really, really understand this because what children learn early will extend into their adulthood. Whatever the original statement of the parents, it has become a lifelong principle. Therefore, parents should be very cautious to make certain that they impart facts to their children and not give them kiddy jokes because they will believe and store the information almost for life.

Example: My mommy said _____ cures _____. All types of superstitious statements.

The same technique applies to learning. If children are taught age-appropriate or non-age appropriate concepts by a trusted, loving voice, it remains stored without a delete button. Would it not be wonderful if children were introduced to and taught lifelong learning skills and academic benchmarks in the same manner? It is very important that all parents and caregiving adults realize that "teachable moments" (the opportunity for learning) are all around us. Cognitive learning begins immediately after birth. Children are very observant and quite capable of thinking and expressing themselves in a clear and consistent manner. Everything they see, hear, taste, and experience results in a teachable moment. All positive and negative interaction can be resolved in a "teachable moment." Teach them how to "turn situations around" for the good! It is important that parents, guardians, and caregivers guard and make certain that the information the child learned is indeed the type of information that can be transferred into classroom settings and is suitable for public discussions. It will amaze you how much information children know, but are limited in their ability to discuss in group settings at school.

Career Planning: Parents, Observe Their Interest

Many times adults will ask children, "What do you want to be when you grow up?" They will reply giving you various career titles. Parents should observe their children closely to determine their interest level. Each of the learning centers in preschool education represents a strategic professional career.

For example, but not limited to:

1. Art & Crafts—artist, designer, fashion, drafting, interior design, etc.

2. Music—musician, singer, music education, etc.

3. Dramatic Play—performing arts: actor, actress, playwright, etc. Home Living—human services & humanities. Health Care—educator. Food Production—chef. Retail. Family Related Careers—law, etc.

4. Games & Manipulative—mechanical/technical invention, etc.

5. Technology—computers: hardware design, programming, web design, etc.

6. Math—business, banking, accountant, etc.

7. Science—research, medicine, scientist, etc.

8. Library—analyst, librarian, historian, educator, author, publicist, editor.

It is important that parents have equal representation of these items available, at hand-reachable level, for children to explore and develop their talents and skills (intellectual personality) at home. Please know that purchasing new items of equipment is not as important as your children having the hands-on experience. They simply want an opportunity to satisfy curiosity and interest.

Examples of Home-Based Learning Center/Manipulative:

1. Supervised computer—age-appropriate, class-related activities. If the information cannot be

transferred into the classroom, then you may not want to chance them storing irrelevant information in their minds.

2. Children's magazines—Subscribe to age-appropriate scholastic magazines through high school. Subscribe to the magazine related to their career and family news and newspaper article discussion.

3. Scheduled Television Time—preschool early learners' programs, History Channel, Discovery Channel, C-Span.

4. Real Life Musical Instruments—piano, guitar, drums. Even if no formal lessons, just observe them to see who will consistently show interest. That is your "CLUE."

5. Parent-Engaged Opportunities—great conversation "relationship building" opportunities: cooking opportunities, first-aid kits, yard tools, home repairs, auto maintenance, dressing, how to tie ties, cosmetic/grooming, sewing machine, fishing, camping, etc.

6. Home Library & Music—healthy relationships, morals, character building, social laws, spiritual guidance.

Learning Opportunities/Extra Curriculum Outside the Home:

As a result of observing and interacting with their child, parents now have a basis for connecting with their child to create a legitimate high school class schedule. High school classes will now expose your child to further opportunity to connect with your child's long-term career.

Remember: Parents are the Primary Career Coach/Counselor.

Time Management Schedule

A tired, stressed body is an unhealthy body. It is impossible to be effective when stressed and tired. Many of the disciplinary issues stem from stress and the lack of rest. Sometimes students refuse to work and participate, are quick to anger, and have difficulty with thought-challenged activities because they are tired and sleepy. Parents must find a way to lead by example in doing their very best to equip their child with a skill as well as a professional education for the future. We are living in a "stressful period." Learning to prioritize events and your level of participation is "Key" for success. There is a direct relationship between student's anger management, stress, and depression. It is often reflected in low test scores and the need for credit recovery classes.

Here are four family projects parents can create and hold each other accountable for during school days and for future career success.

1. *Family Weekday Schedule*—Design it to meet your needs. It can be made from poster board or written on white paper, and placed on the refrigerator

Task	Time
Chores	_____
Homework	_____
Bedtime	_____

**Give thought to your child's participation in extracurricular activities and part-time jobs.

2. **Monthly Calendar**—Mark "SCHOOL PROGRESS REPORT/REPORT CARD" dates on a large wall calendar. Make certain that you get the report card, discuss it with your child, and immediately change your child's schedule and routine if it is not satisfactory. Accept no excuses—modify and supervise the schedule. Students do not fail their grade at the end of the school year, they fail each report card evaluation one at a time. Nip it in the bud! Get close to the teacher and find the missing link.

3. **Weekly Calendar**—Mark special events and work schedule to allow adjustments when needed.

4. ***Daily Assignment/Agenda***—Mark written assignments for classes, tests, and projects.

Home Learning Environment

This is a "RED FLAG" statement in this section geared strictly to the parents. I strongly suggest that you research the multiple learning styles: Visual Learner, Auditory Learner, and Tactile Learner. Everyone learns differently. Children differ from each other just as

Parents: The Primary Career Coach

parents differ from children. Once you research this information, have a discussion with your child, and ask your child's teacher for suggestions, you will realize that the studying area, your home, will make a world of difference in your child's studying and ability to retain information.

It is a district expectation that teachers identify each student's learning style and maintain a classroom environment that allows students to concentrate and engage in class discussions. Sometimes this is referred to as "school climate." Examples: Temperature, lighting, safety, no smoking environment, quiet or very low instrumental and concentrating type of music, uninterrupted focus time. It is very important that when students go home, there is a basic system in place to allow them to complete and retain the assignments for the next class day. Many parents express the demand for their students to have good grades, but sometimes the support system for obtaining good grades could be misleading or not understood. Students NEED the assistance of their parents not only to maintain the respect level of household members, but also the participation of household members/parents in helping the student.

Important Fact: *Parents may not be knowledgeable in the subject area but there are numerous contributions parents can make to encourage integrity for the assignment: Students will try harder if they feel they have a partner.*

Parent Contributions That Encourage Integrity for Completing the Assignments

1. Parents review and hold students to the homework/study schedule.

2. Parents insist on student writing assignments in assignment notebook. Parents read it each day & check it off for completion.

3. Parents—please be respectful and sensitive to your child's assignments and scheduled tests in regard to other family events on the same night, such as church services and other events.

4. Parents have neighbors, visitors, and friends respect children's weekday studying time.

5. Parents notice that friends behind closed doors may not be studying effectively.

Parents: The Primary Career Coach

6. Parents make certain that the work is completed correctly and neatly, that it is legible, clean, and with no food stains.

7. Parents and child review child's work together for correctness or retained test information.

8. Parents have child place work in book bag before going to bed, in a central location, with supplies and lunch money, ready for tomorrow.

Chapter EIGHT

Leadership in Action, Graduation

*"Do what you don't want to do now,
so you can do what you want to do later!"*

Freedom or having free time is great. There is nothing like enjoying relaxation in a great atmosphere with your favorite people. At other times, enjoying quiet private moments can also be enjoyable, with no alarm clocks and no place where one must go. This hardly describes the daily lives of most people, but does characterize features of a wonderful vacation. Vacation is a unique word that suggests that it is a given moment or period of temporary leisure. Once this moment or period has passed, then it is back to the day as usual. Very few things in life have continuous "free gratification." Sacrificial efforts must be applied to finances, certain events, and lifestyles.

We are living in a society where finance is associated with every decision made: type of car to drive, clothes to wear, type of apartment to live in, community, wedding, honeymoon, number of vacations, to own-lease-purchase? Finances are the foundational concern. Now is the time to determine your level of sacrifice required to meet your financial goal.

Three Words To Describe Love: Money $ Money $ and Money $

Play Now, Pay Later. No Pain, No Gain! It is difficult as a student to sacrifice while others are enjoying! How you choose to spend your time could be your most valuable decision: studying vs. playing; homework vs. games; staying in vs. going out; school supplies vs. new clothes & shoes; hair, nails vs. school fees.

Will just getting by or achieving the bare minimum be acceptable to you? If an item cost $99.00 and you have only $100.00, is getting $1.00 change that "cool"? Would you feel more secure having $1,000.00 with extra cash for rollover expenses? Will "coming off the edge" give you a different perspective on just getting by? To remain a law-abiding citizen seeking a preferred lifestyle, you must be willing to make the sacrifices now, and enjoy the benefits later.

Why are teens so intrigued by fashions in high school, allowing other students to make them feel inferior or ashamed? Why is it necessary that students try to fit into certain stylish groups? Most of the time those who desire exterior acceptance (appearances) have very little interior qualities to offer (knowledge, respect, business skills, etc.) More than likely, they will not be affiliated with any of these individuals after high school. Why not create some personal proverbs to strengthen your values and goals? Better yet, clothe yourself with garments of motivation for your future.

Example: You may laugh at me now, but I bet you won't be laughing at me later!

Career Preparation

It is very important that parents assist students in identifying their career interest area. Once this has been established, then students should work with the school's guidance counselor to enroll in all suitable courses that will connect them to the professional area of their choice for college. It is also important for your parents to read the parent or student handbook to learn about the various clubs and student organizations your school offers. You should determine which organization is associated with your career interest level and pursue that organization. This affiliation is very important for processing a resume and application for student employment as well as college entrance applications.

A Personal Career Assessment Site for Students: *www.Facesoflearning.net* (free, printable individual student learning profiles with recommendations.)

Mentoring

Volunteering is an essential aspect of career preparation. Many students are able to obtain several fast food, food service, and retailing employment opportunities. Students who have mainstream professional goals may experience difficulty for entry level employment. Therefore, it may be to the student's advantage to observe a professional person/business person in a field in which the student has an interest.

Mentors are all around us. Parents and other family members are your most valuable mentors. You are able to spend more hours together, whether in person or by telephone. The student should feel at ease in discussing and asking questions as well as spending supervised quality time in exploring career opportunities or information.

Employability skills should be the focus point of every parent for their children from toddler stage through adolescence. Academic preparation is necessary for school entrance at every level: preschool, elementary, middle, high school, and college level. The business and industry sectors of our communities are firm in their request for students who possess employability skills.

Examples of Employability Skills in Demand:

Problem solving—Adapting to new ways of doing things.

Leadership—Able to take responsibility for your actions, helpful, inspiring, flexible, creative.

Teamwork—Able to balance your desires for the good of the team.

Communication skills—Using oral, written, graphic, and electronic communications, being attentive and a good listener.

Creative thinking skills—Able to ask the non-ordinary questions. Can see problems from many angles. Not closed-minded.

Organizational skills—Ability to make plans. Making a schedule. Keeping resources and documents in order. Remembering reports and projects to meet deadlines.

Technical skills—Always being able to show willingness to learn and showing proof of previous classes.

Work Experience

Work experience is very important if you are working hours and days that do not interfere with your academic success at school. Parents should supervise the type of work you apply for, meet the employer, and know their work schedule. It is of utmost importance that your parents honor and encourage you to demonstrate the above employability skills because your performance will be reflected in future job references and sometimes linked to a classroom grade.

Being irresponsible in character, not coming to work, etc. will follow you. Words/conversation travel fast! Build a great reputation and it will attract others to help you and cause them to refer you.

Portfolio

A portfolio is an organized folder that contains all necessary documents to confirm the qualifications of an individual: letters of recommendation, pictures, awards, resume, certificates, national test scores, transcript, newspaper articles, etc.

All parents should make certain that their student is preparing a portfolio by the tenth grade. This will allow ample time for collecting and processing data. Parents should always feel free to contact their child's school counselor to ask for assistance in getting the help needed to format the portfolio. We are living in a very mobile society. Therefore, never underestimate the value of a positive, professional relationship. If your child experienced an outstanding, professional relationship with an adult, help your child prepare a request for a letter of recommendation. Use the sample letter included in this chapter. Once you have received the letter, make copies, and place them in your portfolio file. A character letter of recommendation is just as important for it showcases your young adult's personal qualities and work ethics.

Your Career Summary
Conclusion

"Do what you don't want to do now, so you can do what you want to do later!"

Your Professional Portfolio May Include:

- *Professional resume*
- *Three letters of recommendation*
- *Three professional and one personal recommendation*

- *Copies of awards, honors, community service hours*
- *Photos, newspaper clippings, other documentation of completed projects.*
- *Vocational-technical training records*
- *National state test results*
- *Transcript of completed courses*

Sample Resume
(1–2 pages)

Your Full Name
Address
City, State, Zip Code
Your Contact Telephone Number
Your Business Contact Email

Objective: I appreciate the opportunity to obtain a professional education at _____ College/University. I am very impressed by the integrity and success rate of your students and the guidance and support made available to students.

Education:
   Ready Made Academy, 1999–2004
   374 Mill Road
   Columbus, Georgia 36709
   (000) 000-0000

Work/Volunteer Experiences:
   Company, Dates
   Company Address
   City, State, Zip
   Current Phone Number
   Supervisor:
   Responsibilities:

Special Training & Awards:
Title of Award, Date
Organization
Date

School Clubs and Organizations:
Name of Club or Organization, School, School, Date

References: *(Always adults and not your friends)*

Professional—Certified personnel: Your ability to perform the job (Always include your counselor & teacher)

Personal—Personality qualities and work ethics.

Name, Position
Company or School
Address
Contact Phone/Email

Sample Letter of Application

Mr. John Doe
XYZ Company
P.O. Box 333
Joy Valley, WI 38984

July 31, 2011

Dear Mr. Doe,

I am submitting this letter of application to acknowledge my interest in the _____ position. I believe that my skills will have a positive impact on your company. I am an _____ (example: assertive, dependable, honest, responsible, caring, loyal, punctual) individual and will be an asset to your company. I would appreciate an interview at your earliest convenience and may be reached at this number _____.

Thank you in advance for any consideration given.

Sincerely,

Your Name

Sample Letter of Resignation

Mr. John Doe
XYZ Company
P.O. Box 333
Joy Valley, WI 38984

July 31, 2011

Dear Mr. Doe,

I am submitting this letter of resignation to give my two weeks' notice for the position as _____. I appreciate the employment opportunity from your company. This position has contributed to my professional growth, and I thank you.

As of _____ (date) I will no longer be reporting to work. I wish you all much success.

Sincerely,

Your Name

Your Career Summary

Sample Follow-up Letter

Mr. John Doe
XYZ Company
P.O. Box 333
Joy Valley, WI 38984

July 31, 2011

Dear Mr. Doe,

I am submitting a follow-up letter to you acknowledging my continued interest in your _____ position. I believe that my skills will have a positive impact on your company. Please be reminded that I am an _____ (example: assertive, dependable, honest, responsible, caring) individual and believe that I will be an asset to your company. I would appreciate an interview at your earliest convenience. I can be reached at this number _____.

Thank you in advance for any consideration given.

Sincerely,

Your Name

Sample Request for Letter of Recommendation

Mr. John Doe
XYZ Company
P.O. Box 333
Joy Valley, WI 38984

July 31, 2011

Dear Mr. Doe,

I am submitting this letter, requesting a letter of recommendation for _____. I have enjoyed having you as my _____ teacher and hope that I will be able to implement the many skills learned in your class.

Thank you in advance for your time and effort in preparing this letter.

Please address this letter and mail it to the address below by _____ (date).

Person Name, Position
Company/Institution
Contact Address

Optional: Email/Phone

Sincerely,

Your Name

About the Author

I am a native of Columbus, Mississippi now residing in metro Atlanta, Georgia as a high school educator and published author. My professional degree is in Family and Consumer Science/Home Economics Education, MUW and further studies at MSU. My teaching experiences transcend various developmental stages: Curriculum coordinator and lead teacher for pre-K & kindergarten, middle school and high school educator, college-based daycare certification trainer. I remain active in my community and family ministry. I am a divorced mother and a proud parent of two MSU students: one graduate, one senior and Eagle Scout, plus two wonderful grandsons.

My experience as an early childhood entrepreneur and youth/adult educator gave me the opportunity to develop a close relationship with parents. I was able to observe and walk with them through their daily challenges. I discovered that many of their hearts were in the right place, but some lacked time management skills and a support system for alternative means. Once a strong support system was developed and in place, we became family in words and deeds.

School Readiness for Parents and Children, K–12 is written suitable for all parents and educational programs: home school, public, or private schools. This book simply takes parents straight to the point and alerts them to the *"Proactive Essentials"* for a successful school year. This book is written in a "teacher-friendly voice" to communicate some critical facts to parents. This book cuts to the chase and instantly highlights issues that require parents' immediate attention. As a result of reading this book, parents will be encouraged to work with the school staff by accepting and applying the information given.

As parents and teachers collaborate on their efforts, the student will become excited and motivated for participating in positive learning opportunities in the classroom. *School Readiness for Parents and Children, K–12* contributes to creating a positive and responsive school climate. All educational programs and support groups will want to implement this book as part of their educational plan. It will certainly get the community involved by creating

About the Author

an atmosphere of inclusion for all cultures and nationalities. Make this year your most effective and engaged school year ever!

Your Author and Educator,
Wanda J.R. Prowell

Appendix
Web Site Resources

John Rosemond
www.rosemond.com/parenting

What's Your Learning Style?
http://people.usd.edu/~bwjames/tut/learning-style/

Personal Learning Style Survey
http://people.usd.edu/~bwjames/tut/learning-style/stylest.html

A Personal Career Assessment Site for Students:
www.Facesoflearning.net (free, printable individual student learning profiles with recommendations.)

CPSIA information can be obtained at www.ICGtesting.com
Printed in the USA
LVOW061143110712

289646LV00001B/2/P